LANCASTER AT PLAY
LEISURE IN LANCASTER COUNTY, PENNSYLVANIA

Lancaster County Historical Society

Acknowledgments

The Lancaster County Historical Society extends its thanks to Michael L. Abel, FLCHS, for his time and devotion to producing this volume; our many friends who donated photographs to our collections; and volunteers Patricia B. Keene, Ph.D., and J. Roger Stemen for their years of dedication to the Photograph Collection.

Front cover: Cooling off in Mill Creek, circa 1914. See page 40. LCHS 1-08-08-01
Previous page: The Windsor Ten on a Picnic, July 6, 1916. See page 55 for details. LCHS 1-09-03-02
Back cover (clockwise from top right): Lancastrians on a night out. See page 117. LCHS D-02-03-06; enjoying drinks at the Elks Club. See page 92–93. LCHS 2-12-01-38; beating the heat in an old metal washtub. See page 57. LCHS 2-12-02-17; a fishing trip in Clay Township. See page 33. LCHS 2-12-02-25; baseball in Strasburg. See page 60–61. LCHS 2-12-02-44; Frank Pope swallowing goldfish. See page 123. LCHS 2-01-04-16; the Wild Cat at Rocky Springs. See page 88-89. LCHS A-09-02-77.

Project Manager: Marianne Heckles
Editors: James T. Alton; Thomas R. Ryan, Ph.D.
Design: Michael L. Abel, FLCHS
Printed by Cadmus Communications, Ephrata, Pennsylvania

ISBN 978-0-9740162-5-2
Library of Congress Control Number: 2007935886

Published by Lancaster County Historical Society
230 North President Avenue, Lancaster, Pennsylvania 17603
www.lancasterhistory.org

Contents

Foreword — *Thomas R. Ryan, Ph.D.* — *v*

Introduction — *M. Alison Kibler, Ph.D., and Mollie Ruben* — *1*

Everybody Loves a Parade — *William E. Krantz* — *13*

   Celebrate Good Times! — *Marianne Heckles* — *24*

The Great Outdoors — *Heather S. Tennies* — *29*

The Architecture of Swimming Holes — *Barry R. Rauhauser* — *39*

   The World's Largest Pool — *Marianne Heckles* — *48*

Family Fun — *Heather S. Tennies* — *51*

Sports: History's Other Ten Percent — *Barry R. Rauhauser* — *61*

   Who Stole Second? The 1943 Red Roses — *Barry R. Rauhauser* — *78*

A Day at the Park — *John Ward Willson Loose, FLCHS* — *81*

   A Roller Coaster Ride Through History — *Marianne Heckles* — *88*

At the Club — *Marianne Heckles* — *93*

Dinner and a Show — *Marianne Heckles* — *105*

After Hours — *Marianne Heckles* — *121*

Contributors — *131*

About Our Sponsors — *132*

Photo Donations — *134*

Index — *135*

The Lancaster County Historical Society thanks the following businesses for their generous support of this book:

Sustaining Sponsor

Supporting Sponsors

Contributing Sponsors

Dutch Gold Honey • Goodville Mutual Casualty Company

Foreword

The enthusiastic response to the first two volumes in this photographic history series has been most gratifying. Thank you for your comments, letters and, on occasion, your corrections! Our first volume: *Cars, Trains, Buggies and Planes: Transportation in Lancaster County, Pennsylvania*, received a prestigious Award of Merit from the Pennsylvania Federation of Museums and Historical Organizations. In this, the third volume in our series, we turn our attention to how we spend our time in leisure pursuits. *Lancaster at Play* is a fun look at the seemingly countless ways Lancastrians have entertained themselves and sought recreation from the demands of work and life's responsibilities. Although we don't spend as much time playing as we do working, the time we do devote to fun and recreation is central to living a balanced life. The old adage: "all work and no play make Johnnie a dull boy (or Jane a dull girl)" still holds true.

Photographs have an immediacy that puts us directly in touch with the past. Unlike diaries, letters, or other written records, photos bring us visually into familiar yet foreign spaces and place us inside the long-gone historical moment. We ponder a single photo for hours searching for clues and hints, opening our senses to multiple layers of meaning. Through the magic of chemicals, paper, and light, photographs draw us in to their black-and-white world and temporarily steal us away.

With this third volume in our series of images from the collections of the Lancaster County Historical Society, we offer you a glimpse of people at play in Lancaster County over the years. These images represent the best of the more than 15,000 photographs preserved for all time in our collections. The entire collection is available for your viewing pleasure with the click of a mouse at our headquarters on the corner of Marietta and North President Avenues. We will be glad to make high-quality reproductions of any of our images for your personal enjoyment.

Like our other collections, the Photograph Collection continues to grow through new acquisitions, gifts, and an occasional purchase. Maybe you have old photos of Lancaster people and places that you would like to see preserved for future generations. With a strong commitment to chronicling the history of twentieth-century Lancaster County we are very interested in adding such images to our collection. That is why we are here—to chronicle the history of our communities, to preserve the memories of people who have called Lancaster County their home, and to make these precious pieces of the past easily accessible for everyone to learn from and enjoy. If you would like to donate a photo, please call us at 717-392-4633, and let us know.

Thank you for continuing this photographic journey with us into Lancaster's past. Stay tuned for future volumes in this series. Who knows—you just might find someone you know staring back at you from the past!

Thomas R. Ryan, Ph.D.
President and CEO
Lancaster County Historical Society

Introduction

M. Alison Kibler and Mollie Ruben

From left: Nancy Miller, Mary Ann Brill, Jackie Miller, Dot Miller, Pauline Brill, and Bud Brill have some fun at Maple Grove pool, circa 1943.
LCHS A-10-01-53

Lancaster's leisure has often been idyllic and uplifting. Lancastrians enjoyed picnics by the scenic Conestoga River, dazzling Broadway stars at the Fulton Opera House, and the athletic grace of professional baseball players. But, over the past century, leisure also became serious business in Lancaster. Debates over sexual morality, censorship, and racial segregation mark the history of Lancaster's leisure. A shift in the central location of commercial leisure—from urban to suburban—was also controversial. In the early twentieth century, the city of Lancaster had a thriving nightlife: People strolled the streets, attended theaters downtown, and rode trolleys to amusement parks and other attractions just outside of the city. After this peak of public, urban activity, leisure in Lancaster tended to retreat to individual families' living rooms and backyards.

Around the turn of the twentieth century, more Americans than ever before began to participate in organized sports and outdoor recreation and to patronize commercial leisure venues in American cities. By 1900, for example, there were 10 million bicycles in use, as opposed to 1 million in 1893. While there were no amusement and baseball parks in 1870, by the early 1900s these attractions had sprung up in every city and town in the country. Whereas leisure in the 1870s and 1880s was divided between highbrow and lowbrow venues—between elite pursuits such as opera and "sporting" activities like the smoky, bawdy concert saloons—twenty years later leisure was popular for a much larger, diverse audience.

GOING OUT

The history of Lancaster's premiere theater, the Fulton Opera House, demonstrates the growth of commercial leisure. Established as a community center on North Prince Street in 1852, Fulton Hall became the Fulton Opera House after extensive renovations in 1873. Close to the nation's theater hub in New York City, it drew national stars, including Harry Houdini, Ethel Barrymore, and George M. Cohan. The leading African-American stars of the day, such as comedian Bert Williams and opera singer Sissieretta Jones, also performed at the Fulton. These shows attracted white and black spectators, but the Fulton, like other large northern theaters, probably maintained segregated seating, with African-American patrons relegated to the gallery, the cheapest section of the house.

The Fulton was part of a burgeoning theatrical world in Lancaster around the turn of the twentieth century. The Imperial theater (East Orange and Christian Streets) opened in 1896; the Woolworth Roof Garden, offering vaudeville, launched its inaugural season in 1900; and the Colonial Theater, at North Queen and Chestnut, also competed with the Fulton. The Fulton Opera House underwent its second major renovation in 1904, probably as a response to the rise of other theaters. At the time, the Fulton bookings were set by the Theatrical Syndicate, a group of New York entrepreneurs who controlled theater routes across the country.

Rocky Springs amusement park began as a scenic picnic spot on the banks of the Conestoga in the second half of the nineteenth century. Lancastrians relaxed on the shore and boated and swam in the river. Church missionary groups often held their picnics on the grounds of Rocky Springs. In the early 1900s Rocky Springs expanded to include roller coasters, a shooting gallery, and a dance hall, among other offerings. One of the park's most memorable attractions was an ornate carousel carved by Gustav Dentzel, a German craftsman from Philadelphia. The Dentzel carousel, with its distinctive menagerie of animals, including a rooster and a greyhound, was noted both for its fun and artistry.

Known as wholesome, family entertainment, Rocky Springs reportedly attracted women as

School students from all over the county marched in the Lancaster School Safety Parade. The annual parade through the city of Lancaster honored safety and community at local schools. These high school girls carry the American flag during the 1940 event.
LCHS A-10-01-34

more than half of its clientele. The park, for example, claimed that it was "Lancaster's Miniature Coney Island With all the Objectionable Features Left Out." This kind of promotion was a common strategy used by leisure entrepreneurs in the early 1900s. Promoters of popular entertainment turned to women, previously discouraged from seeking amusement outside of family or church boundaries, as they tried to expand their audiences. The owners of amusement parks, vaudeville theaters, and movie houses argued that their theaters were safe and educational for women and tried to convince patrons that their establishments complemented women's family obligations. In the process, they had to transform the masculine identity of their leisure enterprises. Leisure entrepreneurs barred prostitutes, limited the consumption of alcohol, and tried to curtail obscene performances.

In these ways, commercial leisure was actually on the cutting edge of dramatic changes in women's lives. The nineteenth-century doctrine of domesticity and passivity for white women was crumbling by the end of the century. Women pursued higher education and employment in greater numbers, the movement for women's suffrage gained momentum, and women expressed new assertiveness in dance halls, movie theaters, and amusement parks.

The boys of St. Paul's Lutheran Church in Penryn camp in Israel Bomberger's meadow along the Hammer Creek near Lexington during the summer of 1936. Pictured kneeling are Bobby Frey and Harold Galebach. Standing are Herbert Fry, John Nestleroth, and Isaac Long. Sunday school teacher Harry Bomberger stands behind the boys. LCHS 2-12-02-24

A young school teacher in Lancaster, Mary Eleanor Hoak, exemplified the changes to women's work and leisure in the early twentieth century. She was a single, professional woman who took advantage of expanding night life in the city. She visited Rocky Springs, where she enjoyed a concert by John Philip Sousa, and the Fulton Opera House. In her diary she described her fatigue after a night's "dissipation" at the theater. Hoak also liked going to the movies and meeting friends at ice cream shops and drug stores in town. Adventurous and independent, Hoak even took a trip to New York City, including Coney Island, before moving there to attend Columbia University in the late 1920s.

LAW AND ORDER

The growth of leisure was troubling to moral reformers because of the sexual liberalism of much urban nightlife. The Woman's Christian Temperance Union, for example, advocated more than abstinence from alcohol. It also promoted programs to keep children out of dance halls and

Frank Reiker took over the Lion Brewery about 1870 and built a fine brewing empire. The Reiker Star Brewery soon expanded along the 600 block of West King Street and included the Western Market Hotel, seen here circa 1890. Alex Gerz, brewmaster, and Frank Reiker lean on the bar, perhaps discussing the latest brews. LCHS A-08-02-54

movie theaters and supported federal censorship of motion pictures. Chicago passed the first movie censorship regulations in 1907, and ten years later, many municipalities and states had censorship boards that reviewed films prior to exhibition. Many states also set up anti-vice commissions.

In step with this national trend, Reverend Clifford Gray Twombly, the minister of St. James Episcopal Church, advocated strict movie censorship and established Lancaster's anti-vice organization—the Law and Order Society—in 1911 to clean up crime and immorality in Lancaster. At this time, despite Lancaster's reputation as a conservative, religious city, investigators noted that it was "wide open" for vice. Police were well aware of the extensive network of prostitutes in the city, lawyers even helped run the brothels, and some politicians and businessmen frequented prostitutes. Focusing mainly on prostitution, by 1924 the Law and Order Society had helped close sixty-five houses of ill repute.

The Law and Order Society cast its net wider than prostitution as well. Its investigators scrutinized immorality at theaters, the county fair, parks, dance halls, and skating rinks. It disapproved of the "obscene shows on the midway" at the county fair, stopped teenagers from dancing "indecently" at dance halls, and declared that it was not right for girls to sit on boys' laps at the crowded trolley stops late at night. Its investigators also tried to rescue "charity" girls on city streets—young working women who were willing to exchange sexual favors for a restaurant meal, tickets to the movies, or other gifts. In December of 1920, the Law and Order Society asked the manager of the Fulton Opera House to stop his bawdy burlesque shows. When he refused, the Law and Order Society had him arrested.

The Law and Order Society focused mainly on sexual impropriety, but several theatrical productions and movies were censored in Lancaster because of racial strife. One controversial play in Lancaster was Thomas Dixon's *The Clansman*, which depicted black men threatening white women, freed slaves disrupting democracy, and the Ku Klux Klan saving the South from the disruption of Reconstruction. Lancaster's mayor, J. P. McCaskey, denounced the play because it maligned African Americans and misrepresented Thaddeus Stevens, one of Lancaster's greatest citizens. The play was scheduled for the Fulton on November 12, 1906, but the manager, Charles Yecker, agreed to McCaskey's request to cancel the play. About ten years later, *The Birth of a Nation* (the film version of *The Clansman*) also ran into trouble in Lancaster. The Law and Order Society previewed the film, the Negro Waiters Association objected to the film, and local white politicians again protested against the insult to Thaddeus Stevens.

PLAYING GAMES

Reformers did not just worry about the risqué temptations of leisure; they tried to offer healthy alternatives, such as playgrounds and organized sports. Playgrounds, their supporters argued, could deter crime, Americanize immigrants, and help create an orderly city. Thanks to increased funding, the number of playgrounds in American cities doubled in the early twentieth century. Physical education teacher James Naismith created the game of basketball when faced with a wintertime gap between football and baseball. Basketball spread rapidly through YMCA channels as well as colleges. Lancaster's YMCA, established in 1854, and the YWCA, which opened in 1889, both used recreation to improve the mental and physical wellbeing of Lancaster citizens.

Baseball also began to consolidate and expand in the late 1800s. When the National and then the American League formed in 1876 and 1901, respectively, new standards and policies were made to control ticket prices, schedules, and player contracts.

Baseball's farm system, initiated by Branch Rickey in the early twentieth century, allowed organizations to develop a large quantity of average players into quality major league players. Several minor league teams played in Lancaster in the twentieth century. Although the Maroons (1896–1899, 1905) were a winning team, they lost money every year and disbanded as a result of economic hardships. Next the Red Sox formed in 1932, followed by the Red Roses. Around this time stadium lights and radio broadcasts helped professional baseball around the country, but Lancaster's teams still struggled, playing intermittently between 1932 and 1961. Although Lancaster never had a Negro League team, the Lancaster Giants, in 1887, were Lancaster's only entirely African-American team. Today, Clipper Magazine Stadium hosts large crowds to watch the Lancaster Barnstormers, part of the Atlantic League of Professional Baseball Clubs, Inc., formed in 1998. The league attempts to bring a high level of professional baseball and affordable leisure to communities without major league and minor league teams.

Aletha and Gladys Hess share the drinking fountain in Buchanan Park, circa 1921. LCHS 2-12-02-06

Significant social transitions after World War II dramatically reshaped leisure. Suburbanization undercut urban amusement as baseball stadiums moved out of major American cities and multiplex cinemas became fixtures at suburban malls. The crowds of the early twentieth century stayed away from urban amusements, perhaps unwilling to cross the racial divide that increasingly separated the suburbs from the perceived dangers of the city. The rise of television contributed to an increase in private, family amusements. By 1955 approximately sixty-five percent of American homes had a television. By 1990 the total value of videotape rentals exceeded the entire box office receipts for movies in the United States.

Nancy Tanger, second from left, and her sister, Peggy Neff, second from right, enjoy a Memorial Day picnic with family at Lime Spring Farm in Rohrerstown in 1944. LCHS S-01-05-45

As a result of a gift from Harry M. Musser, the city of Lancaster opened picturesque Musser Park, near the center of the city, in 1949. The creation of Musser Park resembles most other parks in Lancaster, which were established by individual benefactors, not city or county government. The park's garden and small playground remained in good shape for several decades but, when Lancaster, similar to other urban areas, experienced budget cuts, the park began to decline in the 1970s. Some neighbors remember that the city no longer paid for a full-time gardener, and vandalism also became a problem at the park in this period. Like other urban parks, Musser Park suffered from the declining investment in urban areas after World War II. In 1982 the Musser Park Civic Association met for the first time to begin to address the needs of the park. A public-private partnership has undertaken many improvements in the park since the 1980s.

POOL POLITICS

From 1950 until about 1970, the number of swimming pools in the United States increased from nearly 8,000 to more than 100,000. In Lancaster County alone, approximately 2,000 backyard swimming pools were up and running by May, 1959. Instead of buying a second automobile, Americans invested in backyard pools that ranged in price from $2,900 to $8,000. In 1960,

Lancaster had several pools, both private swim clubs with membership policies and privately owned pools that were open to the public, where swimmers would pay an entry fee for access to the pool. African Americans were not welcome at any of them. The exclusion from the Rocky Springs pool was particularly painful at the annual Coatesville Picnic, a large gathering of African Americans from Coatesville, Lancaster, and surrounding areas. At this major social event the amusement park rides were available to all, but the pool was always "closed for repairs."

African Americans, who sometimes learned to swim at the YMCA or YWCA with white elementary school classmates, usually swam in natural bodies of water—either the "Old Poggy" or the Water Works, both in the Conestoga. Five public wading pools, for children under ten, were also available to African-American swimmers in the city. This pattern of segregated swimming in Lancaster fit state and national trends at this time. African-American and white children could usually swim together, and white and African-American students shared the pool at J. P. McCaskey High School, where the classes were single-sex. But for teenagers and adults racial segregation was the rule—explicit or unspoken—when men and women swam together.

In the midst of suburbanization and efforts at urban renewal, Lancaster civil rights activists began to challenge segregated swimming in the area. The National Association for the Advancement of Colored People (NAACP) and the Freedoms Committee, a group of Lancaster progressives focused on civil liberties, turned their attention to three privately-owned pools: Brookside, Maple Grove, and Rocky Springs. These pools were ostensibly open to the public for a fee, but African Americans were not allowed. The Freedoms Committee first tried to get the pools to admit African Americans voluntarily. When that did not succeed, the Freedoms Committee asked Robert Pfannebecker, a recent graduate of the University of Pennsylvania's law school, to file lawsuits against the three pools for violating the state's public accommodations law. He won all three lawsuits, but the pools did not immediately open their gates to African Americans. The owners of Rocky Springs leased the pool to the Lancaster Order of Moose to avoid integration, and the pool closed with the rest of the park in 1966. Maple Grove Recreation Association sold the pool

Twenty-year-old Harvey Williams gets ready to lap the competition in his finest racing gear, circa 1898. Williams was owner of one of Lancaster's most famous and longest running cycle shops. By the 1950s, you would have been hard pressed to find someone in town who didn't own a Harwilco bike. LCHS MG-62 The Johnny Houck Collection

Marietta's sluggers lined up for this shot, circa 1915. LCHS 2-12-01-44

to become the Maple Grove Country Club with limited membership, probably to avoid desegregation. After initial resistance, Brookside and Maple Grove eventually desegregated before they closed.

Dissatisfied with Rocky Springs' resistance to civil rights, the NAACP organized several protest marches in the summer of 1963. The marchers carried signs saying, "We're walking for our rights," "Our color won't wash off," and "Prejudice handicaps our nation." Theresa Robinson, a student who participated in the protests, proclaimed, "The time is right for everyone all over the United States to show people that we want equal opportunity.... Through demonstrations we are showing the way." She further explained, "We swim together at school [McCaskey], so I don't see why we can't swim together outside" at Rocky Springs.

Two years later, the NAACP marched again, this time to advocate for the construction of a public pool for Lancaster. The president of Lancaster's NAACP, The Reverend A. L. Stephans, described the purpose of the march: "to dramatize the unrest and concern of the non-white community about the lack of public recreation facilities in the city, especially the lack of a swimming pool, to give the Lancaster community the opportunity to become more greatly concerned about the problem and to see the persons who are most affected by the lack of public facilities, and to give the community an opportunity to think about potential immediate solutions to the problem." The protests proved successful. On August 8, 1966, the city's first public pool, Conestoga Pines, opened on the Water Works property near Eden Manor. Although the pool still remains about one to two miles away from the southeast section of the city, it has always been open to all people, regardless of race. Lancaster County followed the city and built a larger public

pool in Williamson Park in 1967. After nearly ten years of hot summer months, the efforts and protests for truly public pools in Lancaster proved successful.

LANCASTER LEISURE: LOST AND FOUND

The shift from the amusement park of the early twentieth century to the corporate theme park nearly one hundred years later reveals fundamental shifts in leisure. The amusement park was primarily urban, drawing local audiences with public transportation, but corporate theme parks catered to suburban, middle-class audiences and attracted national and international audiences. Theme parks offer clean, well-coordinated entertainment, rather than the haphazard, and sometimes risqué, collection of rides and performances at traditional amusement parks. Media conglomerations now use theme parks to announce new products and promote their images internationally.

Hershey Park, founded around the same time as Lancaster's Rocky Springs, became a theme park after World War II. In 1977 Rocky Springs owners invested a million dollars into renovating the entire park in an effort to compete, but in that same year Hershey Park paid two million dollars for the first looped roller coaster on the East Coast. With its national brand recognition, Hershey Park could follow the models established by the Disney parks and Six Flags attractions, and by the late 1970s it began to attract more than a million visitors each year. Rocky Springs never outgrew the era of the old-fashioned amusement park. It declined and closed for good in 1980.

The opportunities for play in Lancaster have certainly expanded in the last century—from picnics and dips in the river to movies, amusement parks, and television. Although many have memories of carefree fun in Lancaster, the county's leisure was not always fun and games. Throughout the twentieth century, business owners, moral reformers, and civil rights activists understood just how serious play could be.

These gentlemen may be workers at Frank Reiker's Star Brewery in Lancaster, circa 1885. Whether they were celebrating a special occasion or just a fine keg of beer is not known. Frank Reiker may be the man seated to the right of the keg. LCHS 2-10-01-09

John Kevinski and his dog pause at the weighlock on the canal at York Furnace during a Susquehanna River fishing trip, circa 1889. Kevinski taught in Lancaster City's public schools for many years. LCHS 2-01-01-23

SELECTED BIBLIOGRAPHY

Tyler L. Greiner. "A History of Professional Entertainment at the Fulton Opera House, 1852–1930." M.A. thesis. Pennsylvania State University, 1977.

William F. Hartman, M.D., "From Wide Open to Tightly Closed," *Susquehanna Monthly Magazine*, Dec. 1980, pp. 32–37.

Phillip Jenkins, "A Wide-Open City: Prostitution in Progressive Era Lancaster." *Pennsylvania History*, Vol. 65, 1998. pp. 509–526.

M. Alison Kibler, Lisa Richman, and Randi Weinberg, "The Fulton Opera House in Black and White: African American Performance and Protest in Lancaster, Pa, 1890–1915," *Journal of the Lancaster County Historical Society*, Vol. 106, No. 2, 2004, pp. 50–67.

John W. W. Loose, "A History of Sin and Vice: Lancaster—The Fallen Angel," *Journal of the Lancaster County Historical Society*, Vol. 94, No. 4, 1992, pp. 105–116.

"Maple Grove Will Become Private Club," *The Lancaster New Era*, 31 Jan. 1963, pp. 1–2.

David Nasaw, *Going Out: The Rise and Fall of Public Amusements*. New York: Basic Books, 1993.

"Pool Protest March Today," *The Lancaster New Era*, 16 June 1965, pp. 1, 8.

"Rocky Springs Advertisement," *The Lancaster Intelligencer*, 16 July 1910, p. 4.

David Schuyler, "Musser Park: An Enduring Gift to the City of Lancaster," *Journal of the Lancaster County Historical Society*, Vol. 106, No. 2, 2004, pp. 68–83.

Jeff Wiltse, *Contested Waters: A Social History of Swimming Pools in America*. Chapel Hill: University of North Carolina Press, 2007.

Right: Part of "Theater Row" on North Queen Street was the Scenic Theater, owned by John Peoples. Peoples was quite the entrepreneur. He owned People's Bathing Resort on the Conestoga River opposite Rocky Springs, as well as the *Lady Gay* and her sister paddleboats. The Scenic remained in business until 1930 and is now the site of Lancaster Square. LCHS A-09-02-58

Year 1902
E. King St.,
Westenbergers, Maley & Myers

Everybody Loves a Parade

William E. Krantz

Many communities, schools, or organizations celebrate special occasions with a loosely unified drama or some type of procession, such as a beauty pageant. Two of the largest pageants produced in Lancaster County were historical commemorations. The Pageant of Liberty in 1926 marked one hundred and fifty years of our nation's independence. In 1929, the Pageant of Gratitude celebrated two hundred years since the founding of Lancaster County. More than two thousand people—actors, musicians, and singers—took part in this three-night production at Franklin & Marshall College's Williamson Field.

Parades were held annually in many communities in Lancaster County to observe Memorial Day, Independence Day, other holidays, and the fall farm shows. These parades usually included marching bands and dignitaries riding in open automobiles, sometimes with

escorts standing on the running boards. Merchants or civic groups often provided floats. For several years around 1940, the Lancaster Junior Chamber of Commerce sponsored a Halloween Parade.

When a circus came to town, the troupe usually paraded through city streets with elephants, cages of wild animals, clowns, and possibly a calliope. Over the years thousands of people sitting on curbs or boxes or chairs on city sidewalks viewed School Safety parades, ethnic holiday parades, and Loyalty Day parades which were started during the Vietnam War era to promote patriotism.

From the 1920s to the 1950s, one early autumn evening saw F&M freshmen, clad in pajamas, parading through downtown streets escorted by sophomores with long paddles. This rite of passage for the young men of F&M lasted for several decades, but came to an end as times changed and altercations with locals during the parades became too frequent.

Above: A circa 1942 Liberty Loan parade aimed to drum up support for our boys overseas and the World War II effort. The Armstrong Cork Company adorned its float with the American eagle, among other patriotic symbols. LCHS D-04-04-55

Left: The elephants of Buffalo Bill's Wild West Show lumber down East King Street toward the fairgrounds on Harrisburg Pike. Fans brought chairs onto their roofs to watch the parade on May 20, 1902. LCHS 2-03-07-40

Lancaster's annual county fair came to an end in 1931, by which time air travel was the latest craze. The fairgrounds building is seen in the background as a man maneuvers a blimp over the gathered crowd. LCHS 1-02-03-61

For one week each summer beginning in 1909, Lancaster held a county fair at the city's fairground along the Harrisburg Pike, now the site of R. R. Donnelly and Sons. The crowd in this circa 1910 photo mingles on the midway. Attractions often included a sideshow, like the "Half Man Half Fish" and other oddities. LCHS 3-13-02-21

Spectators gathered on Frederick Street to watch a parade celebrating Millersville's bicentennial on July 4, 1961. LCHS 2-12-02-67

May was usually the month the circus came to Lancaster. The Cristiani Brothers Circus elephants made their way west past the old Hotel Brunswick on Chestnut Street on an unseasonably cold May 15, 1959. The cool weather didn't deter 9,000 countians from showing up to the big top for the festivities. LCHS 1-03-03-38

Above: Cabbage Hill, mostly comprised of Lancaster's Eighth Ward, has always been a tight-knit community. This photograph ran on the front page of the June 16, 1923, *Daily Intelligencer*. The neighborhood gathered for a "Cabbage Hill Celebration and Festival" to celebrate the opening of the new and improved Manor Street. LCHS 2-04-06-10

Left: "April showers us with safety," says the banner carried by Letort Middle School students in the 1961 School Safety Parade. The kids are seen here making their way in the opposite direction on Chestnut Street than the circus parade on the previous page. Buildings on this since-demolished block include the old Village nightclub and Hotel Brunswick in the background. LCHS 2-12-02-66

Budding artist Glenda Galebach gets ready for the Farm Show Parade in Lititz in 1952. LCHS 2-12-02-29

A crowd gathered in Lititz to watch the Community Days Parade make its way along Broad Street in this circa 1950 photo. The three-day festival also included the 4-H Baby Beef Show. LCHS 2-12-02-57

A crowd gathered along the curb of West King Street just past Penn Square to get a good view of the Lancaster Dairyman's Parade in 1939. LCHS A-10-01-22

The ladies of the Lancaster Sanitary Milk Company bundled up for Lancaster's New Year's Day parade in January of 1927. Even snow on the ground couldn't stop this parade from happening. The Sanitary Milk Company later became Penn Dairies and then PennSupreme. LCHS D-12-02-54

Right: Everyone loves the circus, as evidenced by the crowd of kids waiting to see the Hagenbeck-Wallace Show at the Family Theater on the corner of West King and Water Streets in Lancaster, circa 1915. LCHS 2-12-02-48

Marianne Heckles

A h, the Twenties. Our boys were just home from the Great War. The Griest Building reached new heights on Lancaster's skyline. Housing and business boomed louder and better than ever. Bathtub gin abounded. Lancaster finally had a Sunday newspaper. This decade wasn't called "Roaring" for nothing! The county was having a good time—and what better way to celebrate than with a magnificent pageant or two?

The idea of celebrating the sesquicentennial of the signing of the Declaration of Independence originated with the Lancaster County Historical Society. A program committee was formed and the Pageant of Liberty was born. A cast of Cecil B. DeMille proportions paid tribute to our founding fathers by cavorting around in costumes and reenacting key Revolutionary events on Franklin & Marshall College's Williamson Field. The three day affair was held June 5, 6 and 7, 1926.

continued…

Above: The March of Celebration makes its way to Williamson Field during the Pageant of Gratitude. Held June 24-26, 1929, the pageant celebrated the 200th anniversary of the founding of Lancaster County. The young ladies in this photo represent the county's many towns and villages. Among them are Ruth Good (Lincoln), Margaret Savage (Bareville), Florence Eshleman (Pequea), and Sylvia Miller (Kinzer). LCHS 1-02-04-13

Left: This scene from the Pageant of Gratitude reenacts "The First Treaty," the 1744 treaty among the Six Nations and the English, represented by Lieutenant Governor George Thomas of the province of Pennsylvania, just before the French and Indian War. LCHS 2-06-07-30

Revolutionaries get ready for some dancing on Williamson Field during the Pageant of Liberty, July 1926. LCHS D-04-01-77

Festivities included prominent local figures—David Bachman Landis, owner of Landis Art Press, and esteemed Franklin and Marshall professor H. M. J. Klein, to name a few—donning powdered wigs and frilly costumes to portray prominent historical figures. Oh, and don't forget the Fanfare of Trumpets, the Liberty Choir, or the Dance of Joy.

The pageantry didn't end there. Three years later, perhaps in an effort to outdo themselves, the historical society set out to wish Lancaster County a very happy 200th birthday. Again, a cast of thousands gathered on Williamson Field for the extravaganza that was the Pageant of Gratitude. The musical theater retelling of Lancaster County's history compressed 200 years into three days on June 24, 25 and 26, 1929. Again there were funny costumes and musical numbers entitled "O Clap Your Hands!" and "Hail Columbia!".

By today's standards, the costumes may seem historically inaccurate or even politically incorrect. It's almost comical that more people were in the pageants than actually watched them. Yet these events captured the spirit of the 1920s. They partied like it was 1929, and well they should have, because there wasn't much to celebrate by the time 1930 rolled around.

Right: These lovely ladies in their laurel wreaths and Greek goddess costumes prepare for the Diana Dance during the Pageant of Liberty at Williamson Field, July, 1926. LCHS 2-04-05-02

The Great Outdoors

Heather S. Tennies

I n the early days of this country, hunting and fishing were necessary for survival. These skills provided food for the family and furs for the economy. By the late nineteenth century, however, hunting and fishing were considered sports, social activities, and modes of relaxation. The large number of sportsmen's organizations that formed added social components to these outdoor activities.

Sportsmen's organizations were made up of men and/or women, depending on the nature of the club. Members gathered for outings along the Susquehanna River, in the mountains, or at other remote locations. Clubs represented many interests, including hunting, fishing, camping, picnicking, hiking, canoeing, and bird watching.

Newspapers often publicized outings of clubs—and even individuals. J. L. Lyte's fishing excursion with his family to Mill Creek was announced in the *Lancaster Daily Intelligencer* in August 1881. The *Columbia Spy* reported that a camping club of young ladies would be staying at York Furnace for ten days in July 1886, while "one solitary man *continued…*

Above: Roger Hollinger (center) and friends enjoy a trip to the woods, which apparently included some good games of baseball, circa 1900. Hollinger graduated from Lancaster Boys High School in 1899. LCHS 1-05-01-95

Left: Low water below the Safe Harbor Dam allowed M. W. Bair to fish from the rocks of the Susquehanna River. No date. LCHS 1-01-03-70

guards the camp at night. "The same article stated, "All the world is joining a club…Good company, good weather, good location, a good commissary, and good cooks go far to make a week enjoyable, as well as profitable."

Lancaster County woods offered game such as deer and wild turkey, and anglers looked forward to catching trout and bass, but the social aspects of these organizations were just as important as the hunt. One camp on Maiden Creek in Berks County did not allow alcohol or cigarettes in 1886, as it was run with military discipline by prohibitionists. That approach stands in stark contrast to another group's pyramid of beer kegs in 1907 (see page 34). With or without libations, clubs provided camaraderie and a chance to escape from everyday life.

The great outdoors was a lure for youth, as well as adults. Children were introduced to outdoor activities at home and even at school. An 1856 letter from S. Shoch in Columbia to Mrs. Isabella Slaymaker in Gap discloses that the youth of Columbia found rabbit hunting to be good. "Miss Mary [Shoch] is learning the young idea how to shoot…but there is one hand she does not teach—& that is 'how to fish.' What think you of that being added to the school requirements of the fair sex?"

Who can resist an idyllic spot along the Susquehanna River? Sometimes the peacefulness of the site beckons the solitary angler to enjoy an afternoon surrounded by the sights and sounds of nature.

Ladies even participated in the hunting festivities. This woman, possibly Mrs. Anna R. Vogel, shows off her gun in a 1927 photograph. LCHS D-05-01-08

Camp fun at the turn of the twentieth century usually meant live entertainment. The men in this circa 1900 photo gather around to listen to music provided by a fiddle, flute, and cornet. LCHS D-05-03-23

Ruth Bomberger Rose, Alice Keller Galebach, and Robert Biemesderfer head out on a fishing trip in Clay Township in this 1918 photo. LCHS 2-12-02-25

Left: Herbert Beck and friends take a lunch break during an outing in the 1950s. Beck was a professor of chemistry and mineralogy at Franklin & Marshall College. He also gave lectures on ornithology, the study of birds. This photo may show one of his many birding trips. LCHS 2-03-02-16

This 1907 excursion to the woods seemed to revolve around beer drinking, as evidenced by the pyramid of beer kegs and frosty mugs all around. A good time must have been had by all. LCHS 2-10-02-13

Fishing was even a way for couples, like the one seen here, to spend a quiet day together. This couple tries their luck in Chiques Creek, circa 1885. LCHS 2-05-02-17

Hunting has long been a Lancaster County tradition—so much so that schools cancel classes and people take time off work to head into the woods on the first day of doe hunting season. These men and their dogs show off their quarry behind Jacob Wolfer's Golden Eagle Hotel at the corner of King and Duke Streets, circa 1895. LCHS 2-05-02-17

A father-son fishing trip has long been a good way to spend a quiet afternoon. This father and son seem to be doing just that, circa 1925, despite the big catch of weeds they've just landed. LCHS D-02-05-84

The Architecture of Swimming Holes

Barry R. Rauhauser

Artifice and nature must come together in near perfect unison to form a good swimming hole. Nature provides the backdrop: a well-shaded stream bed, cool water, and land and rock formations that momentarily slow the water just enough to provide the width, depth, and security one requires for total submersion. Man provides the rest: stone dams to deepen the waters, rope swings wrapped around steel-strong tree limbs, a grassy shoreline that has been properly abraded by many hundreds of pairs of bare feet, and a"No Trespassing" sign located near enough to give warning, but far enough away that everyone can ignore its notice.

In Lancaster County, such swimming holes earned wide acclaim, often evolving into public gathering spaces, permitting hundreds of swimmers at a time. Michael Trissler built his hotel at Rocky Springs in 1855, and its bathing beach undoubtedly earned a recognizable spot among swimming holes soon after. By the turn of the twentieth century, people took the trolley or the steamboat to Rocky Springs, visiting the amusement park and splashing in the waters.

Likewise, the banks of the Conestoga near the Water Works east of Lancaster City were also inhabited by crowds on hot summer days. Still others found their water habitat in the remains of man-made endeavors, claiming old quarries and mines, where the unknown water-

continued…

By the 1910s, public swimming pools began springing up all over Lancaster city and county. Silas Buckwalter opened Brookside Swimming Pool on Harrisburg Pike in 1914. Bathers seen here in 1930 try to beat the summer heat. LCHS D-02-04-42

filled depths provided a sensation of, if not a very real, danger. In each of these cases though, the swimming holes grew naturally, evolving over many years into a form of recognizable landscape architecture. They often arose slowly, randomly, and unconsciously.

As the twentieth century began, entertainment entrepreneurs took over for nature, crafting large outdoor swimming pools in Lancaster County. Recreating the same watery thrill that their more "natural" counterparts achieved required careful planning. Sliding boards replaced the rope swing, diving boards replaced the worn creekside edge, and admission fees replaced the "No Trespassing" signs. In 1914, Silas Buckwalter constructed Brookside Pool while Ralph Coho opened the floodgates to Maple Grove's two-million gallons of water. These quickly became regional summertime destinations for those wishing to experience a more secure and safe water environment.

Over the years, many others would follow: Locust Heights in Columbia, Ironville's Twin Oaks, Adamstown's Community Pool, Quarryville's American Legion Park. Large and small, private and public—the swimming pool became just as much a part of Lancaster's landscape as the swimming hole.

Cooling off on a hot summer day sometimes means jumping into the nearest body of water. These boys dive into the Mill Creek below Williamson Park, circa 1914. (We assume they checked the depth first.)
LCHS 1-08-08-01

These Lancaster lads and lassies went wading in a creek sometime about 1915. It was perhaps the easiest and definitely the cheapest way to cool off back then. LCHS 1-01-04-24

Kids cool off in "Old Poggy Creek," as one stretch of the Conestoga River was known, in southeast Lancaster sometime in the 1940s. LCHS A-08-02-15

Right: A raft and a water slide were the highlights of the Rocky Springs bathing beach along the Conestoga River. W. J. Wade, at the left end of the raft, and his friends enjoy the river, circa 1910. LCHS 1-01-02-29

Boys practice their balancing act in the pool at Camp Andrews. Floating around on an inner tube, whether in a pool or down a creek, was always a great way to cool off. LCHS 2-12-02-01

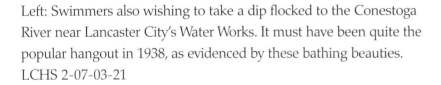

Left: Swimmers also wishing to take a dip flocked to the Conestoga River near Lancaster City's Water Works. It must have been quite the popular hangout in 1938, as evidenced by these bathing beauties. LCHS 2-07-03-21

Robert "Sketch" Mearig didn't even bother to change into his swimming trunks on one hot day in 1938. He just dove right into Lutz's pool in Lititz. LCHS 2-12-02-58

Youngsters enjoy a swimming party at the old lead mines near Swarr Run off the Harrisburg Pike, proving that you could swim almost anywhere in 1910. LCHS A-09-02-11

Friends and family gather at the Charles Long estate at 708 North Duke Street in Lancaster for a Fourth of July swim in 1925. The home and the pool are still standing today. LCHS D-09-01-19

Marianne Heckles

A couple—possibly Isaac Plotnick and an unidentified lady friend— enjoy a day at Maple Grove's swimming pool, circa 1927. LCHS D-02-04-36

Sometime in the 1890s Aaron Summy planted a grove of maple trees on property that had once been a prosperous mill. At the time, the old mill building, erected in 1767 by Johannes Steiner, still stood along Columbia Avenue as Summy took over operation of West End Park.

In 1912, Summy sold the land to Ralph W. Coho, who turned it into Maple Grove Park. Coho, a local business man, built a pool that in 1914 ranked as the largest in the world. It held up to two million gallons of water and had plenty of room for Lancastrians to splash around. He later built a second pool that boasted the title of "Largest in Pennsylvania." It was lined with Belgian blocks once used to pave the city's streets. Coho shipped in sand from Cape May, New Jersey, to make a bathing beach.

He also added the amenities that made Maple Grove a full-fledged amusement park. They included a snack bar and rides, such as the Sky Rocket roller coaster and airplane swings over the pool. He even built an auditorium that served as a dance hall and sports arena. It hosted entertainers such as Benny Goodman, and was the venue for many boxing matches. The park became popular enough to have its own trolley line.

Over time the rides disappeared, but the pool remained a popular spot for people to beat the summer heat. The Coho family sold Maple Grove to Christ and Elaine Hampilos in the 1950s, who kept the pool shipshape. The old mill building became changing rooms. The Hampilos family sold the property in the 1980s, but the pool remained open until 1988.

Today, Lancaster Township owns the park, and the auditorium serves as the township's community building. Johannes Steiner's mill survived hundreds of wet bathers, the flood waters of Hurricane Agnes, and a little rezoning, but was destroyed by fire in 2005. The pool, of course, is history.

Left: Ralph W. Coho built Maple Grove pool in 1914. Maple Grove Park would later include a ballroom and an amusement park with rides, including the Sky Rocket roller coaster. The pool was all that was left when this photo was taken around 1960. LCHS 2-04-03-13

Family Fun

Heather S. Tennies

Some of our fondest memories involve time spent with family and friends. Picnics, family reunions, lawn games, and parties of all kinds are moments that stand out when we look back on our lives or at our family's photograph albums.

Celebrations bring us together with a common purpose, allow us to praise and support each other, and provide forums for traditions to be passed down to younger generations. In July 1818, James Evans wrote to Samuel S. Cochran, "We had a great party on the Island on the 4 of this month." A celebration, however, is not the only reason for families to come together. Simply having beautiful weather may inspire a barbeque or pool party.

Although gatherings are natural opportunities to bring out the camera, families also seize the moment to record everyday events. The 1915 photograph of children playing on bicycles and wagons (page 52) preserves that youthful activity for future generations. The clothing, toys, and expressions

continued…

Above: We don't know who this lady is or where she was—possibly Long's Park or Rocky Springs—but she sure looks like she was enjoying the fun and games at this picnic sometime in the 1920s. LCHS LM-01-01-70

Left: These little girls may have gathered for a proper birthday party for Emily Detweiler, daughter of Armstrong executive Sanderson Detweiler, at the family's home on Marietta Avenue near School Lane Hills, circa 1931. LCHS D-02-05-61

on the faces of the children all contribute to the story told by the image. Little Levi Rudy (right) might have been living his dream of being a cowboy when he dressed up for a pony ride.

Birthdays, anniversaries, holidays, and reunions are particularly well-documented occasions in family history. Photographs of these gatherings, especially family reunions, are often staged, allowing individuals to be identified and hopefully preserving the moment for eternity.

Not all poses, however, are serious and formal. The image of the family adorned by flowers (page 56) suggests an enjoyable picnic. More spontaneous moments are captured in candid shots, which bring life to cherished memories. The child artist and the bathing toddlers are much too cute to leave out of the family album. The time spent with family and friends is preserved in photographs for ourselves and for those who follow.

Top: This gang of kids, with Charles Stauffer second from right, gets ready to take off on an adventure with their wagons, scooters, and bikes, circa 1915. LCHS S-01-03-71

Bottom: What three-year-old wouldn't want a pony ride? Levi Rudy of Howard Avenue certainly enjoyed it back in 1947—just ask the mystery person hidden behind his steed! LCHS A-10-02-01

The men of the Stumpf, Ganse, and Fritsch families—all from Lancaster's Cabbage Hill—gather for an afternoon of fun and music on a summer's day in 1907. LCHS A-09-01-10

The Glassley family gathered at Ferncliffe Cottage near Benton Hollow Creek in Drumore Township for outings in the country. Here they play croquet on the lawn by the cottage, circa 1910. LCHS G-01-02-35

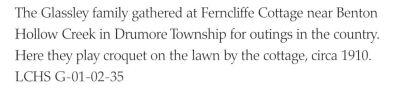

An outing in the outfield seemed like a fun idea for these young people about 1910. An ad for Frank A. Rieker's Star Brewery adorns the outfield wall behind them. The venue could possibly be the Rossmere Ballpark, just east of Lancaster at Juliette and Frances Avenues. LCHS 1-06-03-50

According to Amy Ellen Whitaker's Diary, the date was Thursday, July 6, 1916. It was vacation week for those who worked at the New Holland Silk Mill which was located at Brimmer Avenue and Grant Street in New Holland. "Named ourselves Windsor Ten. Very nice day. A crowd of we girls ten of us went fishing over at Windsor. Took dinner & supper along. Pop took us over. Rutt's four girls [Katie, Clara, Susan and Mary], Viola Lauffer, Helen Ranck, Pearl Spotts, Ruth Fox, Norma [Whitaker] and I." The Windsor Ten got together other times also, as Amy notes, to sew, to crochet, and walk up town. A photo of what is probably the "dinner & supper" mentioned above appears on the title page. LCHS 1-09-03-01

The Simcock family gathered a bit of arbutus during their picnic at Pequea in 1909. Pictured around the table are Mary Simcock, Thomas Simcock, Sarah Simcock, Millie Simcock Turner, Charles F. Simcock, and Grace Simcock. LCHS 2-12-02-12

Sometimes beating the heat meant splashing in an old metal washtub. Lynny and Bruce Herneisen play in their tubs in their backyard in 1948. LCHS 2-12-02-17

The Atwater family, from left, Howe, Jane, Charlotte, Richard and Pierce, get ready for some serve and volley action on the tennis courts in this 1964 photo. LCHS 2-12-02-79

Families gathered around to check out the homemade racecars just before Lancaster's Soap Box Derby held near J. P. McCaskey High School during the 1940s. LCHS 1-09-01-45

Sports: History's Other Ten Percent

Barry R. Rauhauser

Perhaps historians have gotten it all wrong. In their attempts to analyze the past, they have studied our wars and generals, presidents and politics, corporations and CEOs, science and inventors. These are the fundamental blocks of their American stories—the things that have shaped our past and will continue to mold our future.

But, if we are truly looking at America's story, perhaps we should be concentrating more on our first basemen, our quarterbacks, the young duffers who managed a hole-in-one on the Gold Course at Strasburg's Village Green, or the batter who swung at a large white softball tossed in a high arc through a humid August sky—and missed.

The people and events that surround sports may seem trivial when examining the "serious" story of America. But serious historians are indeed beginning to examine this world. The games we play and how we play them tell these historians quite a bit about who we are and who we might become.

continued…

Above: The bathing beauties of the 1941–1942 swimming class get ready to show their stuff at the YWCA Seated from left to right are Dot Shissler, Carol Bagger, Janet Lyons, Ann Edelson, Ruth Snyder, M. F. Sarkasian and Doris Hopf. LCHS 2-12-02-78

Left: It was the bottom of the ninth for Strasburg batter Joe Rineer. Umpire Nelson Wallick and Mountville catcher Warren Evans get ready for the pitch. Strasburg's team was a real powerhouse in 1953 when this photo was snapped. Joe hit nine homeruns that season. LCHS 2-12-02-44

Many might argue that Americans do not place as much value in sports as they do in education, science, or politics. But if one compares the salaries of the best high school teachers with a bench warmer in the NBA—or the number of viewers for the last presidential debate versus the last Super Bowl—a different picture emerges. Sports matter.

There are the athletes. They toss footballs or shoot hoops or swing at baseballs tossed on the grounds of Columbia's Glatfelter Memorial Field. They played on teams organized from members of local branches of the VFW or the American Legion, the YMCA or YWCA, or centered around their local companies, high schools, or universities. Since the nineteenth century they have swung tennis racquets, croquet mallets, and baseball bats. They have traveled across the landscape by bicycle, roller and ice skates, sleds and skis, sneakers and cleats.

There are also the spectators. They watched Leo Hauck box inside the Fulton Opera House, they watched the Hatters in Adamstown, and they watched the cars zoom around the Lancaster Speedway. They cheered on the athleticism as much as the acting of the Mat Maulers—the "professional rasslers" at Maple Grove—and they rooted for the Red Roses, just as today they applaud the Barnstormers.

Here in Lancaster, sports is highly valued. It is as much a part of our daily concern as world events and national debate. Over the past one hundred years our local newspapers have devoted roughly ten percent of their valuable ink and paper to sports, every single day. While many describe Lancaster to be one of America's finest gardens, it is an image that would not be complete without a few geometric lines drawn in white lime across its surface.

Although eating peanuts and popcorn along the third base line is possibly the best way to view a baseball game, the view from the outfield may have been just as impressive during this July 4, 1907, game at Columbia's Reservoir Park.
LCHS 2-12-01-47

Right: The Park Hill gang from Lancaster's Eighth Ward battled Reading's Exeters on the first illuminated football field in Pennsylvania on October 26, 1929. The field was located in Stevens, just north of Ephrata, and the game was only the second to be held on the field.
LCHS 2-12-02-11

Lancaster's Eighth Ward Alerts football team poses for their championship photo, along with their canine mascot, in 1907. LCHS 3-08-03-02

Whether on skis, a sled, or a snowboard, flying down a snowy hill is always fun. These kids in Columbia enjoy a man-made hill on a winter's day in 1875. LCHS LM-01-03-93

What's a little fighting among brothers? The boys in this photo may be the Rittenhouse brothers: David, Samuel, and Jacob. One looks on as the other two prepare to square off behind the family home on South Water Street, circa 1910. LCHS D-03-05-82

A leisurely bike ride through the country is a good way to spend a day, though these gents from the League of American Wheelmen looked like they were up for more of a challenge. The men stopped in Lancaster long enough to pose for a picture in front of the Stevens House Hotel during a tour from New York City to Staunton, Virginia, in 1887. LCHS 2-12-01-14

Curling isn't exactly one of the most popular winter sports, but it was good enough to draw a crowd at Engleside back in 1937. Taking the opportunity to use the frozen Conestoga River for fun, a group of Lancaster business men take up the challenge. LCHS A-08-01-01

Lancaster's Greenwood ball club takes a break for a photo, circa 1910. LCHS 3-10-01-02

The girls of the Northern Lights baseball team pose for their team picture, 1937. Their ball field was located along Keller Avenue where the Days Inn now stands. LCHS A-09-02-38

Warren Close, right, and Larry Ezard, center, hone their archery skills at Camp Shand in 1948. Camp Shand has had many homes since it was established in 1894, making it the third oldest YMCA camp in the United States. When this photo was snapped, the camp was located near Carlisle, Cumberland County. Today campers trek to Cornwall in Lebanon County to reach Camp Shand. LCHS 2-06-07-37

Left: Watchmaker Ezra F. Bowman founded the Bowman Technical School in 1887. Young men from all over the country came to Lancaster to learn watchmaking and engraving skills from Bowman and his sons, John and Charles. The school quickly became a full-fledged educational facility on the corner of Duke and Chestnut Streets. Here, John and Charles Bowman pose with the school's basketball team, circa 1910. LCHS B-01-06-04

George Swain rides Shadowa, a horse owned by Dr. D. Frank Kline, at a horse show at Rossmere Ballpark at Juliette and Frances Avenues, circa 1910. Swain was a horse trainer and drayman at the Union Boarding and Livery Stables, which were located at 218 Nevin Street in Lancaster—now the site of Sacred Heart Catholic Church's parking lot. LCHS 2-06-07-10

With the Hamilton Watch building in the background, these boys enjoy a game of shuffleboard along North West End Avenue, circa 1930. LCHS D-02-03-98

A crowd gathered to watch the Knights of Malta hit the lanes on league night back in 1926. Who knew bowling could be such a spectator sport? LCHS D-02-04-15

The basketball players at Linden Hall School for Girls pose for their team photo in 1925. Located in Lititz and founded in 1742, Linden Hall is the oldest continuously operated school for girls in the United States. LCHS D-01-03-32

A group of circus gymnasts forms a pyramid at the YMCA gymnasium. When this photo was taken in 1921, the Young Men's Christian Association was located at 21–25 West Orange Street, the present location of the Wachovia Bank building. LCHS D-02-05-22

At Donovan's Department Store, 32–38 East King Street, a young woman gears up to hit the links at the store's indoor golf cage. The store, which operated from roughly 1915 to 1930, must have had an excellent sporting goods department. LCHS D-10-04-50

LANCASTER
RED ROSES
1946

THOMAS STUDIO

Barry R. Rauhauser

Under player-manager Elwood"Woody"Wheaton, with star players George Kell, Les McCrabb, and Major Bowles, the 1943 Lancaster Red Roses pulled off a very successful season and took the Interstate League Championship. During their last few regular season games, ticket sales topped 5,000—with more than that in attendance. Soldiers and sailors were allowed in free, as were ladies who brought a donation of half a pound of waste fat.

In the finals of the 1943 Governor's Cup Series, Lancaster faced its rival from across the Susquehanna, York's White Roses. York took the first win, but after six games, including a 14-inning sixth game, the series was all tied up.

Which left game seven. Winner-takes-all. 7,267 fans in attendance. York earned a run in the first inning, but the score remained 1-0 until

the fourth, when York scored three more. The White Roses seemed to be on a roll—until the bottom of the fourth inning.

Then everything went black.

And for good reason: The blackout sirens wailed. Game or no game, everyone's lights dimmed to black, leaving fans and players in the dark. When the lights came on again, things had changed. Wheaton couldn't find his glove, and someone had literally stolen second base.

It took fifteen minutes for play to resume. Wheaton found his glove, and a new second base was brought out onto the field. The Red Roses immediately scored four runs, tying the game at 4-4. Wheaton put Les McCrabb in to pitch the rest of the game, and McCrabb shut down York's hitters.

In the seventh, the Red Roses scored two more. George Kell, Lancaster's most popular player two years in a row, knocked a ball deep into center field to send in the winning run. York managed to plate another run in the ninth but failed to score again.

With their 6-5 victory, the Red Roses were crowned absolute rulers of the 1943 Interstate League.

Above: The 1958 Red Roses have a little fun while posing for their team photo. LCHS 2-11-06-06

Left: Under manager Tom Oliver, the 1946 Lancaster Red Roses went 55 (wins) and 83 (losses) for the season. LCHS 2-09-02-15

A Day At the Park

John Ward Willson Loose, FLCHS

Until late in the nineteenth century earning a living consumed most of the average working man's time. The invention of street cars or trolleys enabled families to begin to visit public parks or seek recreation away from the city.

In Lancaster, two early public parks were the West End Park on the Little Conestoga Creek and Rocky Springs Park along the Conestoga River. Located west of downtown, West End Park was a destination of John C. Hager's West End Horse Car line. By the

continued...

Above: Although known for its world-record-sized pool, Maple Grove Park also had a well-known ballroom. The dance floor hosted many dance marathons like the one advertised on the truck in this 1930s photograph. LCHS D-02-04-51

Left: Chickies Rock has been a popular scenic overlook for generations. Lancaster County officially began acquiring the land for use as a park in 1977. Today Chickies Rock County Park covers more than 400 acres. In this photo taken in 1890, people take in the view of the Susquehanna River and York County in the distance. LCHS 2-04-03-35

1920s, new owners had changed its name to Maple Grove, and expanded the park to include the thrills of a roller coaster and other amusements including a carousel, a tunnel of love, and a swimming pool.

Not to be outdone, Rocky Springs built a larger roller coaster—the Wild Cat—guaranteed to make girlfriends clutch tightly to their boyfriends. In addition visitors could take Captain John Peoples's steamboat, the *Lady Gay*, from Witmer Bridge down the Conestoga to the park. Captain Peoples had a huge slide down into his swimming pool: the Conestoga River. Swimming at the Brookside Pool, just east of Long's Park, was more sanitary, but probably less fun than skinny-dipping in the Conestoga River.

Private parks, such as Wheatland Park between Lampeter and Strasburg, catered to organizational picnics and festivities. Boroughs also offered their citizens park facilities, such as Lititz Springs Park and Manheim's Kauffman Park. In Lancaster and its suburbs, civic-minded persons created Long's Park and Buchmiller Park for the benefit of the community. A bequest by umbrella handle maker H. M. Musser established a park on the old Grubb estate in the city on Lime Street.

Nearly every community had its own "ballpark" and home team, and some also built tennis courts and golf links. Many communities had roque courts—croquet on a hard surface. During the 1920s and 1930s, men throughout Lancaster County enjoyed competing on summer evenings.

Beverly Bixler Wagaman, her two sisters and their friend Dick Eyde pose for a photo by the pond at Long's Park, Christmas 1937.
LCHS 2-12-02-68

Tobias Hirte and his orchestra were among the first people to make use of the cool and shady area known today as Lititz Springs Park. Hirte entertained recovering Revolutionary War soldiers in 1778. In 1818, Lititz held its first Fourth of July celebration in the park, a tradition that continues today. The people in this circa 1900 photograph seem to be enjoying themselves by the springs. LCHS 2-08-01-02

In 1876, Abraham Kauffman donated the tract of land south of Manheim that would become Kauffman Park. The Zion Lutheran Church Sunday School made good use of the park, as seen in this 1895 photograph. Professor William D. Keeny, longtime music and vocal instructor in the Manheim public schools, can be seen in the background by the horse and carriage. LCHS 2-07-02-15

Bathing beauties gather for a pageant at the Buchanan Park pool, circa 1946. The park, located in Lancaster's West End at Race and Buchanan Avenues, has long been the site of childhood recreation—from swimming in the wading pool in summer to sledding down its hill in winter. LCHS A-08-02-44

Proving that baseball truly is America's favorite pastime, these boys hit the lot in what is now Musser Park. The Grubb family's greenhouses along East Chestnut Street can be seen in the background. The greenhouses were torn down about 1940 to make way for a park made possible by a bequest from Harry M. Musser. Musser Park was formally dedicated on July 4, 1949. LCHS A-10-01-21

In this 1930 photo, ladies and gents gather for an evening of dancing at the Wheatland Park Pavilion in West Lampeter Township, along the Pequea Creek. LCHS D-02-03-85

Marianne Heckles

I t started out as just a shady glen near a spring along the Conestoga River. When Michael Trissler bought the property in 1855, he built a two-and-a-half-story hotel and called the shady glen Rocky Springs. Almost instantly, people flocked to the welcoming riverside retreat for picnics and a cool dip in the river. Church groups used it for camp meetings. Fraternal organizations made it an excuse to get together and have fun. Families came for reunions.

By the turn of the twentieth century, the park had taken on new life and a new owner. Owned by Thomas Rees of Pittsburgh, but managed by Herman Griffiths, Rocky Springs began showing signs of becoming a full-fledged amusement park. People could hop the trolley and then float up river on Captain John People's steamboat, the *Lady Gay*, and spend the day lazing in the sun or the evening dancing in the pavilions.

The first figure-eight roller coaster arrived at the park in the 1920s, as did the now famous carousel and a young man named Joseph Figari, who sold shaved ice with flavored syrup. Figari worked his way up and eventually

continued…

Above: Rocky Springs was the scene of social protests on more than one occasion. Evidence of anti-German sentiment during the World Wars could be seen in games like "Knock the Helmet off the Kaiser." LCHS D-02-03-78

Right: Perhaps the most notable ride at Rocky Springs was the Wild Cat roller coaster. Built around 1928 by the Philadelphia Toboggan Company, the ride was the park's main attraction for decades. After the park closed for the last time in 1981, it sat dormant until it was removed in the early 1990s. LCHS A-09-02-77

Rocky Spring's roller skating rink boasted its own organ and organist to provide live music for its many skaters. The rink closed down with the park in 1979 and burned down in the early 1980s. LCHS 2-06-08-04

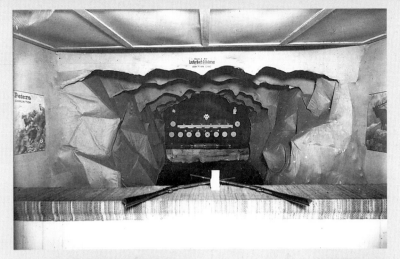

Top: The shooting gallery at Rocky Springs Park was among the many games and rides that brought in the crowds during Joseph Figari's tenure as the park's owner. Mr. Figari bought the park in 1935. LCHS D-02-03-77

Bottom: Keeping in mind less adventurous folks, Rocky Springs offered quiet benches for those who wished just to sit and take in the view of the scenic Conestoga River. LCHS D-02-03-61

bought Rocky Springs Park in 1935. He took the shady little glen to new heights.

Ask any elderly Lancastrian about Rocky Springs and they'll tell you stories of first dates on the Wild Cat or snuggling on the Cuddle-Up. They remember spending hard-earned allowances at the penny arcade or endless afternoons of roller skating. This was the Rocky Springs of the Joseph Figari heyday.

Like any good roller coaster, what goes up must come down. The happy endless summers of swimming pool afternoons and riding the rides lasted until the late 1960s, when park attendance began to dwindle. A brief revival was attempted in 1979, but Rocky Springs failed to spark the imagination of more visitors. The park closed in 1980, and in 1984 the remains of bumper cars and other park paraphernalia were auctioned off. The historic carousel went on its own journey—first to a park in Michigan and then to Dollywood in Pigeon Forge, Tennessee.

The outlook was bleak for Rocky Springs. While the park sat dormant and overgrown for more than a decade, the idea of turning it back into a park of sorts was tossed around. Condominiums had been built on part of the site. Then, in 1999, the carousel returned to Lancaster and brought hope of a new park with it. Today the remaining buildings of Rocky Springs, including Michael Trissler's hotel, have been restored to a bed and breakfast.

The shady glen has come full circle.

At the Club

Marianne Heckles

S ince the dawn of civilization, men and women have been gathering to socialize at the local watering hole. Over time, this socializing evolved into clubs with specific purposes: charity work, recreational activities, hobbies, labor unions, or just an excuse to get together and partake of a beverage.

While some social clubs are nationwide organizations with local chapters, others have their roots right here in Lancaster County. The Slumbering Order of Hibernating Governors—a.k.a. the Groundhogs—was established in 1908 by George W. Hensel, Jr., of Quarryville. Every February 2nd, lodge members gather to witness weather prognosticator Octoraro Orphie, the One True Groundhog. If Orphie sees his shadow, it's six more weeks of winter. If not, it's an early spring.

Another local group is the Pirates Club, also called the Shad Choir Club, which began holding annual shad dinners in 1905. All members don their "piece of eight" before heading off on a "cruise" to many an interesting destination. The Pirates are still swashbuckling today.

Many national associations have had local "lodges" or "airies" in Lancaster County. including the Moose, Elks,

continued…

Above: Perhaps setting out for Tucquan Glen on a summer day in 1889, the Algonquin Club loads up with racquets, rifles, and umbrellas, ready for almost any event. LCHS 2-12-01-38

Left: Enjoying a drink at the club—in this case, the Elks Club, circa 1940—was always a nice way to cap off an evening. The Improved Benevolent and Protective Order of Elks Conestoga Lodge #140 was established about 1915. Today their lodge is at 452 South Duke Street in Lancaster. LCHS A-08-02-90

Eagles, and Lions. While some of these chapters have declined in popularity, the Conestoga Elks Lodge #140 has been going strong since 1915 and has occupied the same lodge on South Duke Street since 1923.

Starting in the 1930s, blue-collar workers from the Hubley Manufacturing Company looking for a little unity gathered at the Hubley Club for an after-work drink. The club still boasts a decent membership more than 30 years after the company closed its doors.

Not to be outdone, the women of Lancaster founded the Iris Club in 1895. The club established its headquarters at 323 North Duke Street and has since performed various charitable functions for the women and children of the community.

Social clubs may revolve around a common goal or cause, whereas others seek to unite like-minded individuals. Any way you cut it, these organizations have been providing a sense of camaraderie and fellowship for many generations of Lancaster Countians.

Lady golfers at the Lancaster Country Club take a break on the porch after finishing up on the back nine, circa 1950. LCHS 2-12-02-54

Ferdinand Demuth, second from left, and the Lancaster Camera Club trekked all over with their box cameras and tripods about the turn of the twentieth century—evidence that personal photography was fast becoming a new fad. LCHS 2-06-07-20

Nothing says summer fun like a game of quoits or horseshoes. The men of the Tucquan Club get tossing at their clubhouse along the Susquehanna River, circa 1930. LCHS 1-04-04-12

Left: At the time of this Press Club outing along the Conestoga River in 1905, Robert B. Risk was president of the club. Risk was associate editor of the Lancaster Examiner newspaper. Hopefully, these newspapermen caught more than one fish and had a little fun on their excursion. LCHS 2-02-02-52

Men of the Order of the Buffalo posed for the camera during a camping trip, July 13, 1889. LCHS 2-03-04-23

The Quarryville Bay Club lines the decks of the steamboat *Dandy* in this 1889 photograph. The club was headed to the Chesapeake for its annual bay excursion. We hope the gentleman perched on the side didn't fall overboard. LCHS 2-06-07-16

The Pirates gather for their annual shad dinner along the Susquehanna River, circa 1910. Harry S. Williamson, founder of the Pirates, is seated front and center. LCHS A-09-03-02

The groundhog lodge makes their way out to the fields to see if Orphie sees his shadow—a longstanding Lancaster County tradition. If the groundhog sees his shadow it means six more weeks of winter. If not, we get an early spring. Unfortunately, Octoraro Orphie is not known for his accuracy. LCHS D-02-04-64

Eagles' Park was a small wooded area along the Conestoga River near the Lancaster City Water Works, behind what is now Deer Ford Estates. The park may be the site of this circa 1900 photograph and the Eagles Club's long afternoon outings. LCHS 3-08-04-01

On June 22, 1909, the Shad Choir Club held its first outing at Upland Lawn, the School Lane Hills home of Harry S. Williamson. Members of the Choir, also known as the Pirates, still get together for "cruises" and shad dinners at the Tucquan Club in York Furnace. LCHS 3-08-02-01

Dinner and a Show

Marianne Heckles

Dinner and a show. It's probably been the most common way to spend an evening out for the last century. For Lancastrians, this meant donning formal wear and heading to the Fulton Opera House for a bit of theater. Built in 1852, it was originally called Fulton Hall. Blasius Yecker took it over and renamed it the Fulton Opera House in 1873. It's been home to performances of all kinds—from minstrel shows to Shakespeare—and has hosted a wide variety of talent, including Ole Bull, the Barrymores, and W. C. Fields.

Concert bands were another popular attraction in Lancaster County. Every town had a band that performed at celebrations, parades, parties, and picnics. Sometimes they just played for the fun of it, and everyone gathered around to take in the sights and sounds. Founded in 1856, *continued…*

Above: Mary Warfel was a patron of the arts and a talented harpist. She was also the daughter of John G. Warfel, vice-president of the New Era Printing Company. She brought many musicians to Lancaster to perform at the Fulton Opera House. LCHS 1-02-03-07

Left: Ray Creamer's Old Time Fiddlers get ready for a hootenanny at WKJC. Owned by the Kirk Johnson Company, the radio station operated in Lancaster from 1920 to 1938. Identified in this 1920s photo are Ray's daughter, Betty, at the microphone; his son Charles, playing the cello; and Ray, seated to the left of Charles. LCHS D-02-03-35

the New Holland Band, the county's oldest and most famous of town bands, continues to wow audiences to this very day.

The silver screen came to Lancaster with the opening of the Electric Vaudeville Palace in 1908. Located at 10 West King Street, it was home of the county's first motion picture theater. North Queen Street, however, later became Lancaster's "theater row," with Dreamland at 43 North Queen, the Hippodrome at 150, and the Hamilton at 166 North Queen. A succession of theaters followed over the years—the Colonial, the Grand, the Capitol—all serving up Hollywood entertainment with hot buttered popcorn for less than a few bucks.

The fabulous '50s ushered in the drive-in age, and teens by the carload could enjoy a night of outdoor entertainment. The Sky-Vue opened on Route 30 East in 1953, the Comet arrived off of Route 283 in 1955 and the Columbia Drive-In on Route 462 began showing movies in 1956. Whether you snuck in through a back fence or went legit on a first date, the drive-in was always the best way to spend a hot summer night. The Sky-Vue closed about 1980 and is now the site of the Tanger Outlets. The Comet passed out of existence in 1979. The Columbia Drive-In, the county's first all-year drive-in featuring automatically installed car heaters, finally went dark in 2005.

Lancaster's last downtown movie theater may have closed in 2000, but that hasn't stopped Lancaster Countians from seeking a good night out on the town. Whether it's a school play, community theater performance, or the latest blockbuster on the big screen, it's still dinner and a show.

Maple Grove was known for more than its pool. At one time the park boasted a ballroom that was home to many local sporting events and big band dances. Seen here about 1942 are Howdy Blankman and his band, accompanied by the lovely vocals of Miss Joanna Bigler Lowry.
LCHS 1-06-02-91

The Lancaster Symphony rehearses for a performance in 1955. A postcard for the 1955 season ticket drive advertised four symphony performances and one "pop" performance during the season. The idea of a local symphony orchestra had been tossed around for decades before it was officially formed in 1947. LCHS 2-03-05-11

It was said that no one could play a banjo quite like Jaky Parks. Seen here with his instrument in 1910, Parks was a regular fixture on Lancaster's city streets. He would often play for meals and could be seen gathering newspapers and rags around town. LCHS 2-01-10-19

Right: Lancaster's Community Theatre staged Broadway favorites like *The Bat* and *Charlie's Aunt* for five years before they disbanded at the beginning of World War II. Here several of the players are shown in a presentation of James Thurber's *The Male Animal* at Edward Hand Junior High School, October, 1941. Left to right: Jack McCartney, Clement Lichty, Pauline Whitaker, Lucille Hauser and Constance F. Anderson. LCHS 2-12-05-67

The boys of the Yeates School practice their swordplay in 1905. Robert Locher is seen, third from left, in a dress. The Episcopal boys' school operated from 1857 to 1930. Its last location was the present site of Lancaster Mennonite High School. LCHS 3-01-03-12

Left: Professor Walter J. Bausman, seen here tickling the ivories in 1891 in his Lancaster studio, graduated from the New England Conservatory of Music. He had studios in Philadelphia and New York City as well. He was the organist for St. James Episcopal Church in 1890 and Trinity Lutheran Church from 1887–1890. LCHS 2-03-01-18

Like most towns across the county, the city of Lancaster claimed its own band. Seen here in 1916, the Iroquois Band was led by conductor Adam Stork from its formation in 1898 until his death in 1938. Identified on this photo at far right is Elam M. Bowman. LCHS 2-06-07-24

The young women of the Lancaster Operatic Society smile for the photographer, circa 1920. Seated at front right is Gertrude Willson, mother of noted Lancaster County historian (and contributor to this volume) Jack Loose. LCHS 3-18-01-03

In 1914, movie-goers rushed out to see Tyrone Power Sr. in *Aristocracy*, advertised in this photo of Lancaster's Hippodrome Theater. The theater was located at 150–152 North Queen Street, now the site of Binns Park. LCHS A-08-02-43

The Conestoga Elks Lodge Junior Herd #148 poses in front of the group's lodge on South Duke Street in the 1950s. The Herd was always ready to show off its parade talent. LCHS A-08-02-16

Clara Jane Bower, second from right, and friends prepare for a Junior League gala, circa 1925. The Junior League was founded in 1923 as a charitable organization and remains active today. LCHS D-02-04-69

These folks get down on their night out, perhaps on their way to a showing of the Rudolph Valentino movie *The Eagle* in the fall of 1925. LCHS D-02-03-06

Lancaster's big singing sensation in the sixties was the Trannells. Pictured here from left are Howard Washington, Chet Stewart, Dave McPhail, Joan Stewart, Ernie Jamison, and Jim Jackson. Their big hit was "Come On and Tell Me." LCHS A-08-02-77

Saturday morning television wouldn't be complete without cartoons and puppets with buck teeth. Kids of all ages enjoyed Percy Platypus and friends on Per-ki Place with Marijane Landis on Channel 8. LCHS 2-12-02-23

After Hours

Marianne Heckles

For most people, the business day ends somewhere around 5 o'clock. The whistle blows, the lights go out, and the workplace grinds to a halt. Thus begins Happy Hour in Lancaster County.

Given Lancaster's history as a brewing town, the city has had its fair share of bars and taverns. Some are college hangouts. At Hildy's at Frederick and Mary Streets, generations of Franklin & Marshall students have dismissed academic stress with a few beers. Others, such as the Blue Star on King Street, have a long history of serving locals. Once known as the Western Market Hotel, the Blue Star became part of Frank Reiker's brewing empire in the 1880s and has kept the brew flowing ever since.

Lancaster's teen scene has had its share of hangouts, too. Local organizations, such as the Young Men's and Young Women's Christian Associations, provided entertainment of all kinds—from soda fountains to teen dances to pool tables. After-school haunts included places like the Dell on West Chestnut Street at College Avenue, where kids put off doing homework while snacking on french fries and Cokes. College kids could snag a soda and some gossip at the student union at Millersville.

continued…

A large crowd at a 1926 costume party celebrates the arrival of 1927. New Year's Eve has long been a popular time to party. LCHS D-02-05-64

Dining out has long been a great way to unwind after a busy day. Today this can be as quick and easy as stopping at the drive-thru on the way home from work. Historically speaking, it may have meant grabbing a bite somewhere like the Delmonico Hotel on Penn Square. The Hall family first opened the eatery around 1903. Though it had many owners over the years, the Delmonico fed thousands of Lancastrians before closing its kitchen about 1970.

Times may change, but one thing remains constant: Everyone needs to blow off a little workplace steam. Whether it's the corner bar or the nearest soda shop or dinner out with friends and family, we all have a special way and place we like to kick back and relax.

These lucky sailors were "In the Mood" for dancing with some of Lancaster's loveliest ladies during World War II. The YWCA hosted many USO dances for local military men. LCHS 2-05-03-18

Right: Frank Pope, Franklin & Marshall class of 1940, swallowed three goldfish on March 29, 1939, and lived to tell the tale. The photo was allegedly taken at Hildy's, a longtime favorite F&M hangout located at Frederick and Mary Streets in Lancaster, but it may actually have been snapped at the Phi Kappa Psi fraternity house, 560 West James Street, where Pope was a brother. LCHS 2-01-04-16

Originally founded in 1889, the Young Women's Christian Association (YWCA) established a branch in Lancaster in 1892. By 1915 the organization had found a permanent location at the corner of Lime and Orange Streets. It fast became a popular hangout for teens such as these, enjoying "short Cokes" in a 1950s photo. LCHS A-08-02-35

The Junior Iris Club wasn't formally organized by Miss Rebecca Slaymaker until 1916, but that didn't stop these young ladies of the club and their dates from holding the first Bal Masque in December of 1914. LCHS 2-04-05-03

The Young Men's Christian Association (YMCA) has a long history of giving boys a place to get off the city's streets. The Y's pool room was a busy hangout when this photo was snapped, circa 1920. LCHS D-02-05-18

These folks hang out with a cold glass of Cherry Cheer, perhaps waiting for their ten cent photos to develop, circa 1915. LCHS D-12-05-18

Patrons of the Delmonico Cafe pause from their refreshments in 1928. A local bar and restaurant on Penn Square, the Delmonico opened about 1903 and served the city of Lancaster for decades. It survived prohibition but not urban renewal and closed circa 1970. LCHS D-10-04-42

J. DeBarry Heinitsh called it the Delicatessen when he opened up his cafe at 678-680 West Chestnut Street in 1911. Since then the corner eatery has multiple incarnations: Delecto Dairies, serving up Penn Dairies ice cream, in the 1930s; and by the 1950s it had become the Dell, a popular high school hangout. Since the 1970s it's had many incarnations and today is Antonio's Pizza House, still a great place to get a soda and a slice. LCHS D-10-04-41

Contributors

MARIANNE HECKLES is a graduate of Kutztown University. She is a research assistant and coordinator of photograph collections of the Lancaster County Historical Society.

M. ALISON KIBLER is an assistant professor of American Studies and Women's and Gender Studies at Franklin & Marshall College. Her research focuses on American popular culture, and she is the author of *Rank Ladies: Gender and Cultural Hierarchy in American Vaudeville*. She holds a Ph.D. in American Studies from the University of Iowa.

WILLIAM E. KRANTZ is a retired Lancaster businessman and a graduate of Franklin & Marshall College. He is a member of the Publications Committee of the Lancaster County Historical Society.

JOHN WARD WILLSON LOOSE is editor-in-chief of the *Journal of the Lancaster County Historical Society* as well as a Fellow of the Lancaster County Historical Society (FLCHS). He graduated from Millersville State Teachers College, now Millersville University, and taught for many years in the Donegal School District

BARRY R. RAUHAUSER is the Stauffer Curator at the Lancaster County Historical Society. He graduated with a B.A. from Penn State University and an M.A. from the University of Delaware's Winterthur Program in Early American Culture.

MOLLIE RUBEN is an American Studies and Psychology double major at Franklin & Marshall College. She will be graduating in 2009. Originally from Hingham, Massachusetts, her family now resides in Rhode Island.

THOMAS R. RYAN, Ph.D., is the president and CEO of the Lancaster County Historical Society. He has a master's degree from the Winterthur Program in Early American Culture as well as a doctorate in American Civilization from the University of Delaware. He has taught at Franklin & Marshall College and Millersville University.

HEATHER S. TENNIES is the archivist at the Lancaster County Historical Society. She holds a master's degree in library science from the University of Kentucky.

About Our Sponsors

Sustaining Sponsor

SUSQUEHANNA BANK

Susquehanna Bank traces its roots back to 1901, when Farmers National Bank of Lititz was founded. As the company expanded and opened new branches, it changed its name to Farmers First Bank and eventually to Susquehanna Bank. In 1982, Susquehanna Bancshares Inc. was created as a parent company for the bank; today, it operates three banks with more than 160 branches in the Mid-Atlantic region, as well as other financial service companies. After more than a century of growth, Susquehanna Bank is proud to call Lancaster County its home.

Supporting Sponsors

KEGEL'S PRODUCE

Kegel's Produce has been providing fresh fruits and vegetables to Lancaster County since the early 1930s, when Paul Checkley, Earl P. Kegel, and James C. Lenox, Sr., sold their wares outside the Lancaster County Courthouse. Today the family business is preparing a fourth generation to supply the region's produce needs.

PAUL RISK ASSOCIATES, INC.

Paul Risk Associates is a third-generation family-run construction services company serving commercial, industrial, and institutional clients in southeastern and south-central Pennsylvania and northern Maryland. Established in 1933 by Donald C. Risk, the company strives to provide quality, cost-effective construction while treating its clients with respect and trust.

RHOADS ENERGY CORPORATION

In 1917 Jerome H. Rhoads began selling kerosene from the back of a rail car in Lancaster County. His business grew to become Rhoads Energy, which today provides not just heating oil but also commercial fueling services and heating and cooling equipment and installation. Its new state-of-the-art building on South Prince Street is helping to revitalize part of Lancaster City.

WILCO ELECTRIC, INC.

Wilco Electric traces its roots back seventy years to Elmer E. Brubaker, who started his electrical business with one truck. Today the third generation of the Brubaker family serves commercial, residential, and datacom customers with thirty employees, twenty-two trucks, and the same belief in quality, customer service, and value that Elmer began in 1937.

DUTCH GOLD HONEY

Ralph Gamber, who founded Dutch Gold Honey with his wife Luella in 1946, invented the plastic honey bear in 1957. Their daughter Nancy helped paint the eyes and noses on early bears.

GOODVILLE MUTUAL CASUALTY COMPANY

A small group of Mennonite men founded Goodville Mutual in 1926 to meet the need for automobile insurance in Lancaster County. The company's vision reflects the Anabaptist beliefs of service and mutual aid.

Photo Contributors

Pauline Whitaker Abel

Richard Atwater

Jim Brenner

Alfred A. Crawford, Jr.

Jeanne DeLong

Noel Dorwart

Jean Eggert

H. Kenneth Fausnacht

Lynn A. Foulk

Kathye M. Fralich

Harold Galebach

Karen Haldeman

Mark Haldeman

Charles Heim

Jim Johnson

Bob Marion

Kenneth Myers

Joe Rineer

Charles G. Schiefer

Page Steele

Cory Van Brookhoven

Barbara E. Witwer

Beverly Wagaman

Angie Lightfoot Roth, Lancaster YWCA.

Index

(*indicates photograph)

4-H Baby Beef Show, 20
Adamstown, 40, 62
Adamstown Community Pool, 40
African American, 2, 4–5, 7
Alerts (football team), 64*
Algonquin Club, 93*
American League (baseball), 5
American Legion, 62
American Legion Park, 40
amusement parks, 1, 3, 9, 48–49*, 81–82, 88–91*, 106
Anderson, Constance F., 108–109*
Antonio's Pizza House, 129*
Aristocracy, 114
Armstrong Cork Company, 13
Atlantic League of Professional Baseball Clubs, Inc., 5
Atwater family, Charlotte, Howe, Jane, Pierce, and Richard, 58*
Atwater, 58*
Bagger, Carol, 61*
Bair, M. W., 29

Bal Masque, 125*
Bareville, 25
Barnstormers (baseball team), 5, 62
Barrymore, Ethel, 2
Barrymores, 105
baseball, 1, 5–6, 8*, 60–61*, 62*, 68*, 69*, 78–79* 86*
basketball, 5, 70–71*, 75
bathing beauties, 44*, 85*
Bat, The, 108
Bausman, Professor Walter J., 110–111*
Beck, Herbert, 32*, 33
Benton Hollow Creek, 54
bicycles, 1, 51, 52*, 62, 66*
Biemesderfer, Robert, 33*
Binns Park, 114
Birth of a Nation, The, 4
Blankman, Howdy (band), 106*
blimp, 14*
Blue Star, 121
Bomberger, Harry, 3*
Bomberger, Israel, 3
Bower, Clara Jane, 116*
Bowles, Major, 79
bowling, 74*
Bowman Technical School, 71
Bowman, Charles, 70–71*
Bowman, Elam M., 112*
Bowman, Ezra F., 71

Bowman, John., 70–71*
Brill, Bud, Mary Ann and Pauline, 1*
Brimmer Avenue (New Holland), 55
Broad Street (Lititz), 20*
Brookside swimming pool, 7–8, 38*, 39, 40, 82
Buchanan Park, 5*, 85*
Buchmiller Park, 82
Buckwalter, Silas, 39–40
Buffalo Bill's Wild West Show, 12*, 13
Bull, Ole, 105
Cabbage Hill, 19*, 53
camping, 29*, 31*, 34*, 98*
Camp Andrews, 45*
Camp Shand, 71
carousel, 2, 82, 88, 91
Celebration, The March of, 25
Channel 8, 119
Charlie's Aunt, 108
Charlotte, 58
Cherry Cheer,, 127
Chesapeake, 99
Chickies Rock County Park, 81*
Chiques Creek, 35*
circuses, 13, 17, 22, 76
Clansman, The, 4
Clay Township, 33

Clipper Magazine Stadium, 5
Close, Warren, 71*
clubs, 29–30, 92–103*
Coatesville Picnic, 7
Cochran, Samuel S., 51
Cohan, George M., 2
Coho, Ralph, 40, 49
Columbia, 30, 40, 62, 65
Columbia Spy, 29
Columbia University, 3
Community Days Parade (Lititz), 20*
Community Theatre of Lancaster, 108*
Conestoga Elks Lodge #140, 94
Conestoga Elks Lodge Junior Herd #148, 115*
Conestoga Pines, 8
Conestoga River, 1, 7, 10, 42*, 45, 67, 81–82, 88, 91*, 97*, 102
Coney Island, 3
Cornwall, 71
costume parties, 121*, 125*
Creamer, Betty, Charles, Ray, 105*
Cristiani Brothers Circus, 17*
croquet, 54*, 62, 82
Cuddle-Up, 91
Curling, 67*

Daily Intelligencer, 19
dance marathons, 81
Dance of Joy, 26
Dandy (steamboat), 99*
Declaration of Independence, 25
Deer Ford Estates, 102
Delecto Dairies, 129*
Delicatessen, The, 129*
Dell, The, 121, 129*
Delmonico Café and Hotel, 122, 128*
Demuth, Ferdinand, 95*
Dentzel, Gustav, 2
Detweiler, Emily, 51*
Detweiler, Sanderson, 51
Diana Dance, 26*
Dixon, Thomas, 4
Dollywood, 91
Donovan's Department Store, 77*
Drumore Township, 54
Eagles (lodge), 94
Eagles' Club, 102*
Eagles' Park, 102*
Eagle, The, 117
Edelson, Ann, 61*
Eden Manor, 8
Edward Hand Junior High School, 108
Eighth Ward (Lancaster City), 19*, 62, 64
Elks Club, 92–93*
Engleside, 67

Ephrata, 62

Eshleman, Florence, 25*

Evans, James, 51

Evans, Warren, 61*

Exeters (Reading football team), 62-63*

Eyde, Dick, 82*

Ezard, Larry, 71*

Fanfare of Trumpets, 26

Farm Show Parade (Lititz), 20

Ferncliffe Cottage, 54*

Fields, W. C., 105

Figari, Joseph, 88, 91

First Treaty, The, 25

fishing, 10*, 29, 33*, 35*, 37*, 55*

football, 5, 62–63*, 64*

Fourth of July, 47, 83

Fox, Ruth, i*, 55*

Franklin & Marshall College (F&M), 13, 33, 121, 122

Frederick Street (Millersville), 16*

Freedoms Committee, 7

French and Indian War, 25

Frey, Bobby, 3*

Fritsch family, 53*

Fry, Herbert, 3*

Fulton Hall, 2, 105

Fulton Opera House, 1–4, 62, 105

Galebach, Alice Keller, 33*

Galebach, Glenda, 20*

Galebach, Harold, 3*

Ganse family, 53*

Gap, 30

Gerz, Alex (brewmaster), 4*

Glassley family, 54*

Glatfelter Memorial Field, 62

Golden Eagle Hotel, 36

golf, 77*, 82, 94

Good, Ruth, 25*

Goodman, Benny, 49

Grant Street (New Holland), 55

Great War, 25

Greenwood ball club (baseball), 68*

Griest Building, 25

Griffiths, Herman, 88

groundhog lodge, 101

gymnastics, 76*

Hagenbeck-Wallace Show, 22

Hager, John C., 81

Hall family, 122

Halloween Parade, 13

Hamilton Watch, 72

Hammer Creek, 3

Hampilos, Christ and Elaine, 49

Happy Hour, 121

Hatters, 62

Hauck, Leo, 62

Hauser, Lucille, 108–109*

Heinitsh, J. DeBarry, 129

Hensel, George W., Jr., 93

Herneisen, Lynny and Bruce, 57*

Hershey Park, 9

Hess, Aletha, 5*

Hess, Gladys, 5*

Hildy's, 121–123

Hirte, Tobias, 83

Hoak, Mary Eleanor, 3

Hollinger, Roger, 29*

Hopf, Doris, 61*

horseshoes, 97*

Hotel Brunswick, 18*, 19

Houdini, Harry, 2

Howe, 58

Hubley Club, 94

Hubley Manufacturing Company, 94

hunting, 29–30*, 36*

Hurricane Agnes, 49

Improved Benevolent and Protective Order of Elks Conestoga Lodge #140 (Elks Club), 92–93*, 94

Independence Day, 13

Interstate League Championship, 79

Iris Club, 94

Ironville, 40

Iroquois Band, 112*

J. P. McCaskey High School, 7–8, 59

Jackson, Jim, 118*

Jamison, Ernie, 118*

Jones, Sissieretta, 2

Hensel, George W., Jr., 93

Junior Iris Club, 125*

Junior League gala, 116

Kauffman Park (Manheim), 82, 84*

Kauffman, Abraham, 84

Keeny, Professor William D., 84*

Kell, George, 79

Kevinski, John, 10*

Kinzer, 25

Kirk Johnson Company, 105

Klein, H. M. J., 26

Kline, Dr. D. Frank, 72

Knights of Malta, 74*

Ku Klux Klan, 4

Lady Gay (steamboat), 10, 82, 88

Lampeter, 82

Lancaster Barnstormers, 5

Lancaster Boys High School, 29

Lancaster Camera Club, 95*

Lancaster Country Club, 94

Lancaster County Fair, 14*, 15*

Lancaster County Historical Society, 25

Lancaster Daily Intelligencer, 29

Lancaster Dairyman's Parade, 21

Lancaster Examiner, 97

Lancaster Fairgrounds, 14–15*

Lancaster Giants (baseball team), 5

Lancaster Junior Chamber of Commerce, 13

Lancaster Mennonite High School, 111

Lancaster Operatic Society, 113*

Lancaster Order of Moose, 7

Lancaster Sanitary Milk Company, 22

Lancaster School Safety Parade, 2*, 13, 18*, 19

Lancaster Soap Box Derby, 59*

Lancaster Speedway, 62

Lancaster Square, 10

Lancaster streets

Buchanan Avenue, 85

Chestnut Street, 2, 17*, 19, 71, 86, 121, 129

Christian Street, 2

College Avenue, 121

Columbia Avenue, 49

Duke Street, 36, 47, 71, 93, 94, 115

Frances Avenue, 54, 72

Frederick, 121, 122

Harrisburg Pike, 13, 15, 39, 46

Howard Avenue, 52

James Street, 122

Juliette Avenue, 54, 72

Keller Avenue, 69

King Street, 4, 13, 21, 22, 36, 77, 106

Lime Street, 82, 124

Manor Street, 19

Marietta Avenue, 51

Mary Street, 121, 122

Nevin Street, 72

Orange Street, 2, 76, 124

Prince Street, 2
Queen Street, 2, 106, 114
Race Street, 85
West End Avenue, 72
Water Street, 22, 65
Lancaster Symphony, 107*
Lancaster Township, 49
Lancaster City Water
    Works, 7–8, 39, 45*, 102
Landis Art Press, 26
Landis, David Bachman, 26
Landis, Marijane, 119*
Lauffer, Viola, i*, 55*
law and order, 3–4
Law and Order Society, 4
League of American
    Wheelmen, 66*
Letort Middle School
    students, 18*, 19
Lexington, 3
Liberty Choir, 26
Liberty Loan parade, 13*
Lichty, Clement, 108–109*
Lime Spring Farm, 6*
Lincoln, 25
Linden Hall School for
    Girls, 75
Lion Brewery, 4
Lions (lodge), 94
Lititz, 20, 45, 75
Lititz Springs Park, 82, 83*
Locher, Robert, 111*
Locust Heights swimming
    pool, 40
Long's Park, 51, 82*
Long, Charles, 47
Long, Isaac, 3*

Loose, Jack, 113
Lowry, Miss Joanna Bigler,
    106*
Loyalty Day, 13
Lutz's pool, 45
Lyons, Janet, 61*
Lyte, J. L., 29
Maiden Creek, 30
Male Animal, The, 108–109*
Manheim, 84
Maple Grove Park, 49, 62,
    81*, 106
Maple Grove swimming
    pool, 1*, 7–8, 40, 48*, 49*
Maple Grove Country
    Club, 8
Maple Grove Recreation
    Association, 7
March of Celebration, 25*
Marietta (baseball team),
    8*
Maroons (baseball team), 5
Mat Maulers (wrestlers), 62
McCartney, Jack, 108–109*
McCaskey, 8
McCaskey, J. P., Mayor, 4
McCrabb, Les, 79
McPhail, Dave, 118*
Mearig, Robert "Sketch,"
    45*
Memorial Day, 6
Mill Creek, 29, 40*
Miller, Dot, Jackie and
    Nancy, 1*
Miller, Sylvia, 25*
Millersville, 16, 121

Lancaster Order of Moose,
    7, 94
Mountville, 61
movie theaters and motion
    pictures, 3–4, 11*, 106,
    114*
Musser Park, 6, 82, 86*
Musser Park Civic
    Association, 6
Musser, Harry M., 6, 82, 86
Naismith, James, 5
National Association for
    the Advancement of
    Colored People
    (NAACP), 7–8
National League (baseball),
    5
NBA, 62
Neff, Peggy, 6*
Negro League (baseball), 5
Negro Waiters Association,
    5
Nestleroth, John, 3*
New England
    Conservatory of Music,
    111
New Era Printing
    Company, 105
New Holland, 55
New Holland Band, 106
New Holland Silk Mill, 55
New Year's Day Parade, 22*
New Year's Eve, 121
Norma, 55
Northern Lights (baseball
    team), 69*
Octoraro Orphie, 93, 101

Old Poggy Creek
    (swimming hole), 7, 42*
Oliver, Tom, 79
Order of the Buffalo, 98*
Pageant of Gratitude, 13,
    24*, 25*
Pageant of Liberty, 13, 26*,
    27*
parades, 13–27*
Park Hill gang, 62–63*
Parks, Jaky, 108*
Penn Dairies, 22, 129
Penn Square, 21, 122, 128
PennSupreme, 22
Penryn, 3
People's Bathing Resort, 10
Peoples, Captain John, 10,
    82, 88
Pequea, 25, 56*
Pequea Creek, 87
Per-ki Place, 119*
Percy Platypus and friends,
    119*
Pfannebecker, Robert, 7
Phi Kappa Psi fraternity
    house, 122
Philadelphia Toboggan
    Company, 88
picnics, i*, 56*
Pierce, 58
Pirates Club (Shad Choir
    Club), 93, 100*, 103*
playground, 5
Plotnick, Isaac, 49*
pool room, 126*
Pope, Frank, 122–123*
Power, Tyrone, Sr., 114

Press Club, 97*
Quarryville, 40, 93
Quarryville Bay Club, 99*
quoits, 97*
R. R. Donnelly and Sons,
    15
Ralph W. Coho, 49
Ranck, Helen, i*, 55*
Ray Creamer's Old Time
    Fiddlers, 105
Reading, 62
Reconstruction, 4
Red Roses (baseball team),
    5, 62, 78–79*
Red Sox (baseball team), 5
Rees, Thomas, 88
Reiker Star Brewery, 4, 9,
    54
Reiker, Frank, 4*, 9*
Reservoir Park (Columbia),
    62*
Revolutionary War soldiers,
    83
Richard, 58
Rickey, Branch, 5
Rineer, Joe, 61*
Risk, Robert B., 97
Rittenhouse, David, 65*
Rittenhouse, Jacob, 65*
Rittenhouse, Samuel, 65*
Robinson, Theresa, 8
Rocky Springs Park, 2-3, 9,
    10, 49, 51, 81, 88–91*
Rocky Springs bathing
    beach, 39, 42, 43*
Rocky Springs swimming
    pool, 7–8

Rohrerstown, 6

roller coaster, 2, 9, 49, 88–89*, 91

roller skating rink, 90*

roque court, 82

Rose, Ruth Bomberger, 33*

Rossmere Ballpark, 54*, 72*

Rudy, Levi, 52*

Rutt (sisters), Clara, Katie, Mary, and Susan, i*, 55*

Sacred Heart Catholic Church, 72

Safe Harbor Dam, 29

saloons, 1

Sarkasian, M. F., 61*

Savage, Margaret, 25*

School Lane Hills, 51

segregated swimming, 7

Series, 1943 Governor's Cup, 79

Shad Choir Club (Pirates Club), 93, 103*

Shadowa, 72*

Shissler, Dot, 61*

Shoch, Miss Mary, 30

Shoch, S., 30

shooting gallery, 91

shuffleboard, 72*

Simcock, Charles F., Grace, Mary, Sarah and Thomas, 56*

Sky Rocket rollercoaster, 49

Slaymaker, Miss Rebecca, 125

Slaymaker, Mrs. Isabella, 30

Slumbering Order of

Hibernating Governors (Groundhogs), 93, 101*

Snyder, Ruth, 61*

Sousa, John Philip, 3

sports, 60–79*

Spotts, Pearl, i*, 55*

St. James Episcopal Church, 4, 111

St. Paul's Lutheran Church, 3

Stauffer, Charles, 52*

Steiner, Johannes, 49

Stephans, Reverend A. L., 8

Stevens, 62

Stevens House Hotel, 66*

Stevens, Thaddeus, 4–5

Stewart, Chet, 118*

Stewart, Joan, 118*

Stork, Adam, 112

Strasburg, 61, 82

Strasburg's Village Green, 61

Street, West Chestnut, 129

Stumpf family, 53*

Summy, Aaron, 49

Super Bowl, 62

Susquehanna River, 10, 28–29*, 30, 80–81*, 97

Swain, George, 72*

Swarr Run (swimming hole), 46*

swimming holes and swimming pools, 6–9, 39–49*,

Tanger, Nancy, 6*

tennis, 58*

Theaters

Capitol, 106

Colonial, 2, 106

Columbia Drive-In, 106

Comet Drive-In, 106

Dreamland, 106

Electric Vaudeville Palace, 106

Family, 22, 23*

Grand, 106

Hamilton, 106

Hippodrome, 10, 114*

Imperial, 2

Scenic, 10, 11*

Sky-Vue Drive-In, 106

theater row, 106

Theatrical Syndicate, 2

Thomas, Lieutenant Governor George, 25

Thurber, James, 108

Trannells, 118*

Trinity Lutheran Church, 111

Trissler, Michael, 39, 88

Tucquan Club, 97*, 103

Tucquan Glen, 93

Turner, Millie Simcock, 56*

Twin Oaks swimming pool, 40

Twombly, Reverend Clifford Gray, 4

Union Boarding and Livery Stables, 72

Upland Lawn, 103*

USO dance, 122*

Valentino, Rudolph, 117

vaudeville, 2

VFW, 62

Vietnam War era, 13

Village nightclub, 18*, 19

Vogel, Mrs. Anna R., 30*

Wachovia Bank, 76

Wade, W. J., 42, 43*

Wagaman, Beverly Bixler, 82*

Wallick, Nelson, 61*

Warfel, John G., 105

Warfel, Mary, 105*

Washington, Howard, 118*

West End Park (Maple Grove), 49, 81

West End Horse Car line., 81

West Lampeter Township, 87

Western Market Hotel, 4*, 121

Wheatland Park, 82

Wheatland Park Pavilion, 87*

Wheaton, Elwood "Woody", 79

Whitaker, Amy Ellen and Norma, i*, 55*

Whitaker, Pauline, 108–109*

White Roses (York baseball team), 79

Wild Cat (roller coaster), 82, 88–89*, 91

Williams, Bert, 2

Williams, Harvey, 7*

Williamson Field, 13, 25, 26*, 27*

Williamson Park, 8, 40

Williamson, Harry S., 100*, 103

Willson, Gertrude, 113*

Windsor (Forge), 55*

Windsor Ten, i*, ii, 55*

Witmer Bridge, 82

WKJC, 105

Wolfer, Jacob, 36

Woman's Christian Temperance Union, 3

Woolworth Roof Garden, 2

World War II, 6, 13, 108

Yeates School, 111

Yecker, Blasius, 105

Yecker, Charles, 4

YMCA, 5, 7, 62, 76, 126*

York Furnace, 10*, 29, 103

YWCA, 5, 7, 61-62, 71, 122, 124

Zion Lutheran Church Sunday School, 84